How Deflation Affects You

Barbara Gottfried Hollander

ROSEN
PUBLISHING®

New York

Published in 2013 by The Rosen Publishing Group, Inc.
29 East 21st Street, New York, NY 10010

Library of Congress Cataloging-in-Publication Data

Hollander, Barbara Gottfried.
How deflation affects you/Barbara Gottfried Hollander.—1st ed.
     p. cm.—(Your economic future)
Includes bibliographical references and index.
ISBN 978-1-4488-8342-4 (library)
1. Deflation (Finance) 2. Monetary policy. 3. Economic development.
4. Finance, Personal. I. Title.
HG229.H6535 2013
332.4'1—dc23

                                                          2012011127

Manufactured in the United States of America

CPSIA Compliance Information: Batch #W13YA: For further information, contact Rosen Publishing, New York, New York,
at 1-800-237-9932.

Contents

Lower prices may seem like a good idea. But is paying less always good for the economy? What if your wages (the price of labor) fall, too? Will you be able to afford those bargains?

Introduction

Imagine walking into a store and your favorite clothes cost even less than they did several months ago. Your first thought is that the clothes are on sale. It must be your lucky day! Then you notice that different goods and services in other stores also cost fewer dollars. The newspapers report that the economy is experiencing deflation. Could this explain the lower prices?

Deflation refers to falling prices throughout the economy. It does not mean lower prices in only one store or one sector (like clothing). Deflation is part of a bigger economic picture. It involves consumers, producers, the government, and the central bank, which is called the Federal Reserve in the United States. Both the government and the central bank use tools to affect the amount that consumers spend, which then influences how much producers supply. The existence or threat of deflation can affect these institutions' policies.

Falling prices may seem good because they reduce the costs of goods and services. But deflation can also be part of a vicious cycle that includes lower company profits, lower salaries, and fewer jobs. For example, during Japan's "lost decade," there was deflation and limited economic growth. By the end of 2001, land values in Japan dropped by 70 percent. This means that a house bought for $100,000 in the 1980s was only worth $30,000 by 2001. Yet, even at reduced prices, people were not willing to spend their money.

Think about a country, like Japan, that experienced falling prices and fewer economic opportunities for more than ten years. Logically, lower prices should encourage consumers to spend their money. After all, there are bargains everywhere! But psychologically, people are afraid to spend. They are earning less money and are uncertain about having their jobs in the future. Therefore, people save their money because they fear the worst. They do not buy all those bargains around them, and companies do not sell these goods and services. This leads to even more economic hardships.

Does deflation always accompany economic downturns, like recessions or depressions? Can a country experience deflation and economic growth? An economy involves many participants, including consumers, producers, and investors both at home and in other countries. The actions and decisions of these market participants, along with government and central bank policies, affect price behavior and economic growth. So the answer to both questions is "It depends." What is certain is that deflation is a global economic phenomenon, which affects people like you.

Chapter 1

Deflation in the Global Economy

"**J**apan used to be so flashy and upbeat, but now everyone must live in a dark and subdued way," said Japanese small business owner Masato Y in 2010. This owner was once part of a middle class that could afford expensive homes, vacations, and luxury cars. But in the late 1980s and early 1990s, Japan's economic growth slowed and prices fell. Twenty years later, Masato Y was still struggling to repay his mortgage. Deflation happens in countries throughout the world. It is a persistent decline in the general prices of goods and services, which can have real consequences for individuals and businesses.

Measuring Deflation

Deflation can be measured by a decrease in the consumer price index (CPI). The CPI describes the average change in prices of a market basket of goods and services paid by consumers living in cities or towns. The market basket consists of items that are commonly used by individuals and families. It includes food and beverages (like milk and chicken), housing (such as rent and bedroom furniture), apparel (like clothes), transportation (such as new cars and gas), medical care (like hospital visits and medications), recreation (such as pets and sports equipment), education and communication (including college tuition), and other products (like haircuts).

Economists compare the changes in the prices paid for these products over time. Then they decide if the price level is rising or falling. Most of the time, the price level in the United States is rising. This means that the American economy is experiencing inflation, or an increase in the general prices of goods and services. For example, from 2009 to 2010, prices rose 1.6 percent. So a cell phone that

ConocoPhillips

Self Serve Gasoline

Regular 4 1 5 $\frac{9}{10}$

Plus 4 2 7 $\frac{9}{10}$

Premium 4 3 9 $\frac{9}{10}$

Diesel #2 4 5 7 $\frac{9}{10}$

Changes in the price of oil also affect gas prices. A 2012 decrease in the oil supply contributed to gas prices of over $4 per gallon (3.8 liters). A car with a 12-gallon (45.4 l) tank cost about $50 to fill up.

cost $100 in 2009 would cost $101.60 in 2010—just from inflation.

Sometimes, the inflation rate slows down. This is called disinflation. Disinflation is not the same as deflation. Disinflation happens when prices are rising more slowly, but deflation is about falling prices. Consider that prices changed by -0.4 percent from March 2008 to 2009 in the United States. This negative number means that the price level decreased—so prices were falling. This was the first deflation in the United States in more than fifty years and was fueled by a drop in oil prices.

Deflation refers to price decreases in different industries. But sometimes, there is a good, such as oil, that significantly influences the consumer price index because it affects many sectors. In the CPI, oil is found directly in products, like gasoline or energy for homes and businesses. Oil is also used to transport goods and maintain businesses. For example, factories transport their goods to stores by truck, plane, or ship, which all use gas. For these businesses, the cost of oil is part of the cost of making their products, so it is reflected in the products' prices. When the price of oil decreases, it can also decrease the costs of these products. From March 2008 to March 2009, oil prices fell and heavily affected the CPI. In fact, if food and energy prices were removed from the CPI during this time, prices actually increased!

Deflation and Economic Indicators

Gross domestic product (GDP) is the total value of all goods and services produced by a country within a period of time,

Annual Percentage Change in the Consumer Price Index

(shown in light blue) from 1997–2009

United States

Prices in the United States are usually rising. In 2012, Federal Reserve chairman Ben Bernanke announced an inflation rate goal of 2 percent.

usually one year. Economists compare GDPs over time to figure out if an economy is growing. To do this, economists have to separate the change in output (such as buying more goods and services) from the change in prices (such as an increase in the costs of goods and services). So they use an economic indicator called real GDP, which is gross domestic product adjusted for price changes. There is also an indicator called the GDP deflator, which can be used to measure changes in prices, like deflation. The GDP deflator examines changes in output while holding prices constant.

The World Deflation Club

An organization known as the International Monetary Fund (IMF) reported that about 25 percent of its tracked countries had deflation in 2009. This was the second-highest number of deflation-affected countries in thirty years. "Economies can recover from deceleration, but it's harder to recover from a deflationary situation," said Lorenzo Amor, president of Spain's Association of Autonomous Workers. "This could be a catastrophe for the Spanish economy."

The Spanish deflation was fueled by business owners, who were desperate to increase their sales. Business owners sell their products at prices high enough to cover their costs. Any additional money is profit. But if owners cannot sell their goods and services, they cannot earn enough money to keep their stores open. At first, business owners looked for ways to cut costs. In Spain, business owners lowered wages and fired many workers. They also lowered their prices in hopes of earning more revenue. Nonetheless, an immediate increase in sales did not follow. "Prices will have to come down more, and we will have to spend less," said Spain's Fermax business owner, Fernando Maestre.

Spain was not alone. In March 2009, wholesale prices in Germany fell by 8 percent, compared to 2008. Other countries, including the United States, Belgium, Portugal, Sweden, Switzerland, and Thailand, also experienced deflation in 2009. All of these countries were still in economic downturns and trying to recover from the global recession.

Rises and falls in GDP describe expansions and down-turns in the economy. This economic cycle also relates to an economic measure of well-being called the standard of living. The standard of living refers to the comfort level that people experience from the availability of goods and services. The United States has a high standard of living because most Americans have access to goods (such as food and housing) and services (doctors' visits, for instance). During downturns, the standard of living decreases; but when the economy is growing, it usually increases.

Deflation and Economic Downturns

Sometimes, deflation happens during a downturn, when the economy is growing slower than before, or not at all. A recession is when total output, or GDP, falls for at least six months. An economic depression is a severe recession, where output is falling by more than 10 percent. When output falls, individuals are buying fewer goods and services, so businesses are selling fewer products and earning less revenue. To cut costs, businesses often fire workers and unemployment rises. Unemployment refers to the number of working-age people who want and are actively looking for work but cannot find jobs. Uncertain about future demand for their products, businesses also decrease other investments, such as building new factories.

During downturns, people have less confidence in the economy and often choose to save more of their earnings. The amount of money earned, after taxes and other deductions, is called disposable income. People have three choices for

Cyclical unemployment happens when people lose their jobs during economic down-turns, like recessions. Job fairs help job seekers to connect with potential employers.

using disposable income: save, spend, or donate. Hard economic times encourage more savings because people are worried about losing their jobs. So they set aside money for possible emergencies, like paying for food and housing when unemployed. When many people begin saving more money, it can further reduce economic growth. This is called the paradox of thrift. It states that more savings mean less spending, which causes the economy to shrink even more.

Deflation can reinforce less spending because consumers may delay spending in search of better bargains. After all, if prices are dropping, goods and services will cost even less in the future. The level of disposable income is mostly determined by income earned from working, also called wages or salaries. For businesses, wages and salaries are the price of labor. Deflation can include the falling price of labor. If incomes fall, people earn less money and have less disposable income. This situation also contributes to less spending, which worsens an economic downturn. During Japan's lost decade (which included deflation and a recession), private-sector wages fell more than 1 percent on average from 1997 to 2003.

Deflation and the Lost Generation

Japan's lost decade refers to the 1990s, when the country experienced stagnation and deflation. Stagnation is a recession that lasts for a long time. Japan's economy had minimal growth, so businesses were selling fewer goods and services. Prices were also falling, so businesses received lower prices for their products and earned less money. As a result, business owners, like Masato Y, were not confident about their economic futures.

During this time, there were also students graduating from colleges and looking for jobs. But little economic growth meant fewer jobs. It was a time known as the "hiring ice age." Many people could not find work. Others took whatever jobs were available, even if they were only part-time or consisted of little pay, such as temporary or contract jobs. In 2007, the number of Japanese that worked as temps (called *hakenshain*) or contract employees (known as *keiyakushain*) increased by about 1.8 million people.

"I've had to lower my expectations a bit," said Sadaaki Nehashi. "But if I had waited around for a full-time job, I might have been waiting forever." This group of people,

According to the first National Survey of Homeless People, Japan had more than twenty-five thousand homeless people from January to February 2003. Many of the homeless built shelters made of waste wood and blue plastic near parks, riverbanks, and roads.

which includes Nehashi, is known as the "lost generation." In Japan, a person's status is partly based on his or her job. After Japan's lost decade, many people with solid educations and skills were forced to take jobs that offered few benefits, low pay, and no job security.

By 2003, the Japanese economy began to grow, but the "lost generation" was still stuck in structural pessimism. They did not believe that their lives would become financially better. Companies that began hiring new employees chose recent college graduates, rather than people who had finished college more than ten years earlier. Many of these businesses felt that the lost generation no longer had the skills needed

Speculative Bubbles and Deflation

In the market, the interaction of supply (the amount produced by businesses) and demand determines price. A speculative bubble is when a good's price increases beyond what people would normally expect in the marketplace. For example, a housing bubble is when the price of real estate (such as houses) rises above what the market can explain. Speculation involves buying or selling financial assets with the goal of making a fast profit, like buying stock and selling it shortly after to make money quickly.

In the past thirty years, many industrialized countries have had speculative bubbles. For example, prior to the lost decade, Japan had both housing and stock market bubbles. From 1970 to 1980, land prices increased 213.4 percent in the six largest cities. From 1980 to 1990, they increased another 251.2 percent, and national land prices rose 119 percent. Japan's stock market bubble involved investments that were assessed at more than their market values.

When a speculative bubble pops, prices of assets drop quickly. In the case of a housing bubble, many people's homes are worth considerably less than their purchase prices. For example, during the housing bubble, Japanese resident Yoshihisa Nakashima bought an apartment for $400,000. He took out a loan for almost this full amount. Then the housing bubble burst. By 2005, his apartment was worth only about $200,000, but he still owed $300,000 in home loans.

After Japan's asset bubble burst in the early 1990s, the country entered the lost decade. In 1992, the annual percentage change in Japan's consumer price index began dropping and hit a negative number in 1995. The CPI's annual change was minimal from 1996 to 1998. Then Japan entered a period of deflation that lasted for seven years. From 2006 until 2008, Japan had little change in the CPI and then experienced deflation in both 2009 and 2010.

for top jobs. By 2007, Nehashi, who graduated with a degree in marine biology, could land a job only as a contractor who sorted packages at a delivery company. He earned one-third of a full-time employee's average income in Japan.

The prolonged recession and deflation affected Japan's lost generation in other ways, too. This generation faced more mental illness challenges. In 2006, they accounted for 61 percent of all depression, stress, and work-related mental disabilities. Few benefits and a lack of job security also led to fewer marriages and number of children. For example, many jobs did not offer maternity pay, where women still receive pay before and after giving birth. By 2006, both the Japanese government and some Japanese companies, like Toyota and Nippon, began helping the lost generation by opening outreach centers, offering counseling, and providing more jobs.

Deflation and Economic Expansions

Most periods of deflation occur during economic contractions, like recessions and depressions. In fact, some economists think that deflation only happens with economic contractions. However, there are examples of economic expansions with deflation. For example, the United States has experienced economic growth and falling prices at least six times since the Civil War, including in 1922, 1928, 1939, and 1955. In all of these cases, deflation occurred in the early stages of economic growth.

There are also cases of deflation and economic growth in other countries. According to the Federal Reserve Bank of San Francisco, Germany experienced deflation or low inflation with a strong increase in real GDP in 1999–2000. China also experienced increases in output with falling prices. From 1998 to 2002, China had deflation and achieved the fastest GDP growth rate in the world, at 7.8 percent per year. Another Asian country, Singapore, also had economic growth and deflation in 2002.

Imagine the economy during these times of economic expansion and deflation. The economy is growing and offering more goods and services. People are employed and earning incomes. Furthermore, all around them, prices are falling, so goods and services cost less. Demand is the amount of goods and services that people are willing and able to buy. The factor that most influences quantity demanded is price. If people are optimistic about their economic futures and prices are falling, they will demand more goods and services. Consumption increases, which reinforces economic growth.

Chapter 2

Deflation in the National Economy

On October 29, 1929, the U.S. stock market lost $14 billion. That week, the market fell a total of $30 billion, which was ten times more than the government spent in 1929. These drops marked the beginning of the Great Depression, which was a large economic contraction that included deflation. An estimated 50 percent of children in the United States did not have adequate food, housing, or medical care. From 1933 to 1934, one out of every four people was out of work. At the end of the Great Depression, the U.S. government and the Federal Reserve became more involved in the economy. Both the government and the Federal Reserve can affect the economy by influencing the spending decisions of individuals and businesses. These spending decisions impact how much an economy grows.

Government spending includes construction projects that provide many jobs. According to the U.S. Census Bureau of the Department of Commerce, public construction spending was $279.1 billion for February 2012.

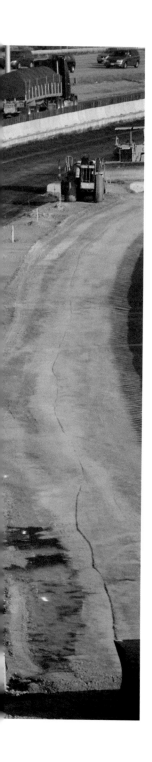

Fiscal Policy

Economic growth is measured by a change in the gross domestic product. Gross domestic product consists of consumption (spending by individuals), investments (such as new homes, factories, and equipment), government spending, and net exports. An export is a good or service sold to another country; an import is a product bought from another country. For instance, Japan exports Honda cars to the United States, and the United States imports them. Net exports equal total exports minus total imports.

The government uses different tools to affect the components of the GDP. For example, local, state, and federal governments can directly raise economic output by increasing their expenditures. When the government pays for roads, public school systems, postal services, and national defense, it is directly putting money into the economy. The government uses taxes to pay for some of its expenses. So taxes are a source of revenue for the government. But for consumers, taxes reduce the amount of money they have to spend.

Suppose you had an after-school job that paid $10 an hour and you worked ten hours a week. Your weekly gross pay is

Deflation, Money Supply, the Great Depression, and Beyond

From 1929 to 1933, the United States suffered through the Great Depression. Both output and prices fell. Many other industrialized countries experienced similar decreases in wholesale prices of 30 percent or more. As prices fell, so did the price of labor, known as wages. Worried that their wages would continue to fall, people were afraid to borrow money since they were unlikely to repay it. Fewer loans led to less spending, which worsened the economic downturn. Believing that they could earn more money in the future, investors also reduced their current investments. During the Great Depression, prices fell about 10 percent each year. Investors believing that they could earn more money in the future also caused current investments to fall.

In the early 1930s, the money supply decreased. By 1932, short-term rates were close to zero. From 1933 to 1937, the Federal Reserve increased the money supply by almost 42 percent, which helped spur an economic recovery. This increase made people believe that prices (including wages) would rise and made them confident that they could repay any borrowed money. As a result, loans and economic activity increased. During these years, prices rose 46 percent. From 1937 until 1949, prices rose again, with a two-month exception in 1939. This 1939 deflationary period was accompanied by an increase in the money supply.

$100. But this is not your take-home pay because items, such as taxes, are deducted before you receive your paycheck. There are federal taxes that Americans pay; there are also state and local taxes that depend on where you live. For example, in 2012, if you earned $100 a week and worked for one year in Michigan, your weekly net pay was about $82, according to SurePayroll.com.

By changing the tax structure, the government affects disposable income and consumption. If the government increases taxes, people have less money to spend. Think about your $82 net pay. If the government increased the tax rate and you only took home $75, you have less money to spend. So increasing taxes decreases consumption and can lead to less economic growth. But if the government decreases taxes, people have more money to spend. This can increase both consumption and GDP. Fiscal policy is the government's use of taxes and spending to affect economic performance.

Fiscal Policy, Deflation, and Economic Booms

During economic booms, people are buying more goods and services and spending more money. Deflation means lower prices, which can encourage people to spend. Buying decisions are based on both present and future expectations. If people believe that the economy will continue to grow in the future, they may take advantage of the lower prices by consuming more today. People are willing to spend because they have confidence in the job market and in their abilities to meet their needs, such as food, housing, and clothing. When businesses are confident about the future, investments (for example, opening more stores) also increase because business owners believe that they will continue selling more products.

If deflation encourages more consumption, it can boost economic growth. Businesses respond by making more investments, which makes the economy grow even more. These investments include hiring more workers and often offering existing workers higher salaries. Both new and existing workers pay taxes, which means the government has more money to spend on goods and services. For example, it can build more roads, buy more computers for schools,

When incomes increase, people buy more of some goods (called normal goods) and less of others (called inferior goods). Most cars are normal goods. When the economy is growing, people are earning more money and consuming more cars.

and hire more teachers. When the government spends more money, it is called expansionary fiscal policy. As previously discussed, this can cause further economic growth by directly putting money into the economy and providing more jobs and services.

Fiscal Policy, Deflation, and Economic Downturns

Now consider what happens when deflation happens during economic downturns, like recessions or depressions. Economic growth has slowed. Businesses are not selling as many products, so they need to cut costs and fire workers. Some people lose their jobs; others are afraid they will. Individuals reduce spending and start saving more money. Even though prices are lower, people are afraid to buy.

On the flip side, business sales are lower and business owners are earning less revenue. Revenue is the amount of money earned from sales. It is calculated as the quantity of products sold multiplied by the product's price. Lower prices and quantities sold mean less revenue. So deflation can make an economic contraction even worse by lowering revenues.

If fewer people are working, tax revenues are also affected. This means that the government has less money to pay for public goods. As a result, it may provide fewer goods and services. This is known as contractionary fiscal policy. For example, the government may choose not to fix certain roads, not to fund music and art programs in schools, or even to close public libraries. Fewer revenues can also affect

Library Closure Notice

All locations of The Seattle Public Library will be closed due to budget cuts

Monday, Aug. 31 - Monday, Sept. 7

The Central Library book drops will close at 8 p.m. Aug. 30 and reopen at 6 a.m. Sept. 8

* Do not leave Library books and materials outside the building during the closure. You will be responsible for theft, loss or damage to Library materials.

* No items will be due and no fines charged or accrued during the closed week.

* If you have book donations, please call the Friends Book Sale Office at 206-523-4053.

Libraries will resume regular hours on Tuesday, Sept. 8.

The Seattle Public Library

The United States experienced a recession from 2008 until mid-2009. According to the American Library Association Office for Research and Statistics (ORS), thirteen state library agencies reported closings in 2009. Other libraries were staying open for fewer hours as a response to budget cuts.

the national debt, which is money owed by the U.S. government.

With fewer revenues, the government may borrow even more money to pay for its expenses. In February 2012, the national debt was already more than $15 trillion! Because of this massive debt, Standard & Poor's downgraded the U.S. credit rating for the first time in history in August 2011. The lower rating can make it harder for the U.S. government to borrow money in the future and may increase the cost of borrowing money from U.S. banks.

Sometimes deflation can even decrease consumption during economic booms. If people believe that deflation will continue, they also believe that prices will continue to drop. So even with the confidence to consume, people are waiting for better bargains. Why buy a product today when it will cost less

America's Saved Decade

In 1991, Japan's lost decade began. More than twenty years later, the country was still recovering. In 2001, the United States' record economic growth ended. Many economists feared that the United States would suffer from deflation, just like Japan did. But it didn't, and some American policymakers thank Japan. "Perhaps because it had learned from Japan's experience, the Fed[eral Reserve] was prepared to implement a vigorous anti-deflationary policy...much more quickly than the Bank of Japan," wrote James Harrigan and Kenneth Kuttner from the National Bureau of Economic Research (NBER).

These NBER researchers cited similarities between Japan and the United States. Both countries experienced recessions after their speculative bubbles popped (like the housing bubble). Both countries eventually lowered interest rates to encourage more demand for goods and services. An increase in demand can raise prices and fight deflationary threats. Harrigan and Kuttner believe that the United States put into action a faster and more aggressive expansionary monetary policy than Japan. Did it avoid deflation? Yes. According to the World Bank, prices in the United States as measured by the consumer price index actually rose each year from 2001 to 2008.

in the future? Therefore, deflation provides an incentive to delay purchases, which also reduces current consumption. As people buy fewer products today, businesses sell fewer goods, which can also reduce future investments.

Monetary Policy

The government carries out fiscal policy by using two tools: spending and taxes. The Federal Reserve enacts monetary policy by implementing different tools: the money supply and interest rates. Money supply refers to the amount of money in the economy at a certain time. There are different definitions for money supply, like M1 and M2. M1 is about money that you can easily exchange for goods and services. It includes cash, coins, and demand deposits (such as checking accounts). M2 includes money that stores value for later use. It consists of M1, plus investment tools, such as savings deposits. Many people put their money into savings accounts, which they later use for college expenses.

One of the jobs of the Federal Reserve is to influence the money supply. For example, the Federal Reserve can increase the money supply by giving banks more money to lend so that individuals and businesses can make big-ticket purchases, like houses, cars, or new factories. Most of the time, they do not have enough money to pay for these items in full. So they pay for part of the cost and then take out loans for the remainder of the balance. A loan is a way to borrow money and then repay it over time. Loans have certain conditions, like a repayment date and an interest rate.

Interest is the cost of borrowing money. It is calculated as a percentage of the amount owed. Interest rates change and

The Marriner S. Eccles Federal Reserve Board Building is located in Washington, D.C. There are also twelve Federal Reserve District Banks throughout the country, from San Francisco to New York.

are determined by the Federal Reserve. When the Federal Reserve increases the growth rate of the money supply, it reduces interest rates. Lower interest rates decrease the cost of borrowing money. Remember that demand for a good usually increases when its price falls. In this case, borrowing money becomes less expensive, so individuals and businesses borrow more money to spend. This occurrence causes both consumption and economic growth to increase.

But when the Federal Reserve decreases the growth rate of the money supply, interest rates rise. This circumstance increases the cost of borrowing money, so individuals and businesses borrow less money. Consumption decreases and economic growth can slow. By changing the money supply and interest rates, the Federal Reserve can affect economic growth. Increasing the money supply is called expansionary monetary policy; decreasing the money supply is known as contractionary monetary policy. This differs from expansionary fiscal policy, which involves more government

Monetary and Fiscal Policy:
What's the Difference?

Policy	Carried Out By	Tools	Expansionary Policy	Contractionary Policy
Monetary	Federal Reserve	Money Supply and Interest Rates	Increase Money Supply and Lower Interest Rates	Decrease Money Supply and Raise Interest Rates
Fiscal	Government	Government Spending and Taxes	More Spending and Lower Taxes	Less Spending and Higher Taxes

spending and/or lower taxes. Contractionary fiscal policy involves less government spending and/or higher taxes.

Monetary Policy, Deflation, and the Liquidity Trap

Both monetary and fiscal policies can affect economic growth. But monetary policy is also used to promote price stability. In fact, some countries view this as its main goal. Their central banks set inflation targets, where prices are only expected to fluctuate within a certain range. Begun in New Zealand in 1990, inflation targeting is now carried out in other countries, including Canada, the United Kingdom, Sweden, Australia, Israel, and Mexico. If prices are expected to rise or fall

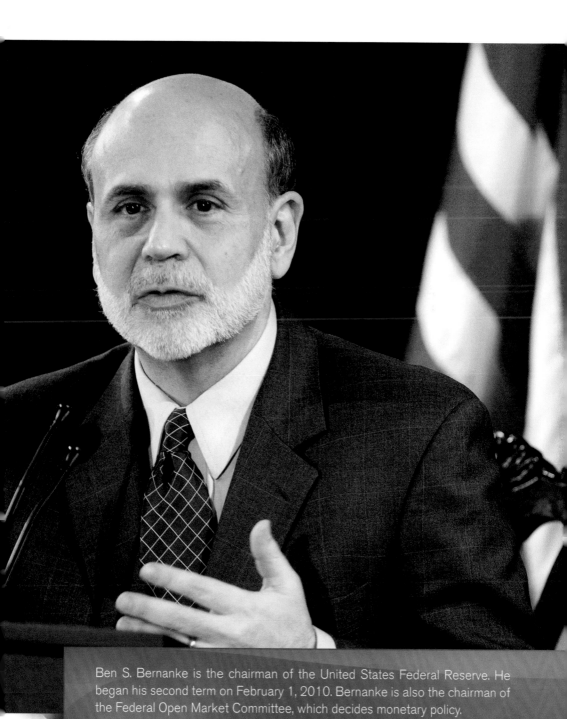

Ben S. Bernanke is the chairman of the United States Federal Reserve. He began his second term on February 1, 2010. Bernanke is also the chairman of the Federal Open Market Committee, which decides monetary policy.

too much, the central banks change the money supply's growth rates and interest rates.

For example, if prices are expected to rise too much, inflation will be higher than the targeted range. So the central bank can decrease the money supply's growth rate to try to reduce expected inflation. Decreasing the money supply and raising interest rates can eventually reduce spending and investments. This lowers the demand for goods and services, which also puts downward pressure on these products' prices. Businesses that are facing less demand for their products also lower their prices to encourage consumers to buy them. But using contractionary monetary policy to reduce inflation often comes at the cost of slowing economic growth.

What happens when prices are falling? Can expansionary monetary policy encourage economic growth and treat deflation? Expansionary policy increases the money supply and lowers interest rates. This should encourage more borrowing and spending. As more people compete for goods and services, this competition puts pressure on prices to rise. So expansionary monetary policy seems like it would treat deflation. But in reality, there have been few opportunities to study the effects of expansionary monetary policy on deflation, since deflation does not occur as often as inflation. However, comparing the effects of monetary policy on prices indicates that monetary policy is more effective in lowering prices than raising them.

Expanding the money supply to raise prices may also pose another problem—the liquidity trap. As defined by the Keynesian school of economics, a liquidity trap happens when interest rates are very low (close to zero), the savings rate is high, and people want to save more money. Rather than encouraging more spending, lower interest rates encourage people to save money because people believe that interest rates will soon rise. When people save their money, they earn interest. This is called the rate of return.

If interest rates are expected to rise, savers will earn higher returns in the future. This encourages people to hold onto their money, rather than spend it. This is especially true if people are risk averse and have little confidence in the economy. Keynesian economists argue that the liquidity trap makes monetary policy ineffective. So expansionary monetary policy, when short-term interest rates are around zero, does not encourage economic growth that could raise prices.

Chapter 3

Impact of Deflationary Causes

Some economists talk about "bad deflation" and "good deflation." When deflation negatively affects economic activity, it is considered bad. It is blamed for less consumer spending, fewer investments, and slower economic growth. But when deflation encourages more economic activity, it seems good. It is credited with increased spending, investments, and economic growth. How can you tell if deflation is good or bad? Find out where it comes from!

Short-Term Positive Supply Shocks

Factors on the supply (or producer) side can lower prices throughout the economy, causing deflation. Businesses want to earn money, so they choose prices that will cover the costs of making their products and hopefully earn profits. For example, suppose that a store sells T-shirts at $5 per shirt. It costs $1 to make the shirt, so a price of $5 allows the owner to cover costs and earn $4 in profit. Now imagine that there was an improvement in productivity or a technological advancement that reduced production costs, such as computers that took orders and processed payments instead of workers. These kinds of improvements lower the costs of producing many products, like clothing, across the economy.

Lower production costs on the supply side are passed along to consumers in the form of lower prices. Remember that price determines the quantity demanded of goods and services. The quantity demanded for most products increases as price decreases. At $5 a shirt, you may be willing and able to buy one shirt. But at $3 a shirt, you may buy two shirts. In a competitive market, businesses lower prices to compete. For example, suppose a store charges $3 a shirt after production costs decrease, but the store across the street charges $8 for a comparable shirt. Most (if not all) people will buy the shirts that cost less. To remain competitive, the store across the street will have to lower its prices, too.

Deregulation and excess supply can also lower prices in different industries. Regulations are rules, usually imposed by the government, that govern behavior. When an industry is deregulated, it has fewer controls. Often, this leads to more competition and lower prices. Industries affected by deregulation include transportation, telecommunications, and natural gas. These industries are factors of production for many goods and services and can therefore affect prices throughout the economy. Economist A. Gary Schilling once wrote, "Deregulation is deflationary," and noted that deregulation in the Australian electricity market caused a 40 percent decrease in its market prices.

The U.S. Airline Deregulation Act of 1978 allowed for an increase in the number of airline companies and lower fares. Before deregulation, the Civil Aeronautics Board decided routes and fares. Since 1978, supply and demand has determined domestic routes and airline ticket prices.

Schilling also discusses excess supply in his book *Deflation: How to Survive and Thrive in the Coming Wave of Deflation.* He notes that businesses around the world can create too many products compared to the number of buyers. Sometimes, like in the 1990s and early 2000s, businesses have access to very cheap financing. They use this money to produce lots of goods, believing that they can sell them in a growing market of buyers. But eventually, people stop buying and businesses are left with unsold products. To cover costs and earn profits, businesses need to sell their products, so they lower prices to boost sales. Schilling notes that "traditional excess supply industries" include "autos, semiconductors, and steel." But in 1991, excess supply was also found in "silver jewelry, cashmere, aluminum cans, blue jeans…golf courses, [and] hotels."

Five Kinds of Deflation and You

In his Forbes.com article, "Deflation Has Arrived," A. Gary Shilling discusses five kinds of deflation: financial, tangible, commodity, labor, and currency. Financial deflation occurs when the prices of financial assets, like stocks and bonds, fall. If your parents have a retirement fund or college fund that consists of stocks and bonds, the value of these funds also falls. This means that they have less money to pay for your college or their retirement.

The second kind of deflation involves tangible assets, or valuable items that you can touch. For example, a house is a tangible asset. It is an investment. You can live in it and pay your mortgage bills, which builds good credit. You can also use your house as collateral when borrowing money. One day, you can even sell your home and earn money. If your home appreciates in value (or is worth more in the future), you can borrow or earn even more money from the sale. But with deflation in tangible assets, your house is worth less than before. In the case of Japan's lost decade, and later when the U.S. housing bubble burst, many people owed more money on their homes than they were worth!

The third kind of deflation involves commodities, or nearly identical goods that can be bought in bulk (such as oil, cotton, or silver). Commodities can be sold directly or indirectly as part of the production process. Therefore, lower commodity prices can lower the prices of products in many industries. For you, it means lower prices for goods and services. Whether or not you take advantage of the bargains depends on the health of the economy.

The fourth kind of deflation occurs in the labor market. Wages fall, and people earn less money for consumption of goods and services.

Finally, Shilling discusses deflation in the currency market. Each country's currency has a value compared to foreign currencies. Currency deflation causes a currency to weaken, which can make foreign goods (such as cars from Japan, toys made in China, and phones from Finland) more expensive. It can also negatively affect trade balances, which influence the economy's health. In 2011, Shilling noted evidence of deflation occurring in all areas in the United States, except for currency.

Good Deflation and You

Businesses lower prices because of improvements in productivity, technological advancements, deregulation, and excess supply. If these lower prices cause a drop in the price level, many economists call the result "good deflation." The short-term supply shocks cause the market to become more competitive, offering lower prices to consumers. People can still feel confident about the economy and spend, and investors are still comfortable with putting more money into the economy. Good deflation encourages economic growth,

During economic expansions, increases in income allow consumers to benefit from falling prices. More spending encourages even more economic growth.

with people buying goods and services at better prices.

Consider how good deflation affects you. Suppose that your parents buy you a used car, but you are responsible for the insurance and gas bills. At first, it costs $40 to fill up the tank. Then gas prices drop. Now it only costs $32 for gas. Deflation means that you have an extra $8 to spend, save, or donate. With lower prices, you can pay the gas bill and enjoy the same benefits from a full tank of gas. But you also gain more benefits from having an extra $8 each time you fill up your car. Supply shocks that increase competition also give more benefits than just lower prices. They offer a greater variety of goods and services and often better-quality goods as businesses compete for customers.

Negative Demand Shock

Lower prices create good bargains and added financial rewards, like having extra money. But when deflation occurs from less demand for goods and services, it can be harmful. This bad deflation comes from people demanding fewer goods and services. It accompanies economic downturns, when people are less confident about their economic futures and are spending less money. Less demand puts downward pressure on prices. Businesses earn less money because they sell fewer products. To cut costs, businesses fire workers. Consumer spending decreases even more, as do tax revenues needed for public goods. Bad deflation reinforces economic downturns and can make it more difficult for an economy to recover.

During the recession in 2008, the popular New York City hot dog chain Gray's Papaya lowered its prices even more to increase sales.

Now consider how bad deflation affects you. Bad deflation occurs with economic downturns, when people are demanding fewer goods and services. Businesses are earning less money, because they are selling fewer products at lower prices. To cut costs, businesses often fire workers. This scenario means that the job market has fewer opportunities for you, your friends, and your family. You will have a harder time finding a job and may know people who have lost their jobs, even in your own family. Worried about their economic futures, people, including you, save more money. Activities and items, like eating out and concert tickets, are no longer necessities. They become luxury goods and services that you can hopefully afford again when the economy recovers. If you do find a job during an economic downturn, you may discover that your wages are lower than you expected. Remember that wages are the price of labor. When deflation occurs, prices drop. Economic downturns also lead to less demand for workers. This situation can mean earning less money, even if you and your family members have jobs. Although prices are lower during bad deflation, you have less money to spend and may be too worried about the future to take advantage of bargains.

Chapter 4

Deflation and Money Choices

Suppose you work at a part-time job for ten hours every week and it pays a minimum wage of $7.25 per hour. Your weekly gross pay is $72.50, but your take-home pay is $60. You believe in only spending what you earn, so you make a budget. Your weekly expenses include $20 in gas, $25 in eating out after school, and $15 for entertainment (like movies and music downloads). Then deflation happens and prices drop across the economy. You still buy the same amount of gas, food, and entertainment. But now, these goods and services only cost $50. This sequence of events means that you have an extra $10 to spend, save, or donate each week. What happened to your money? It has more purchasing power!

Decisions, Decisions

Economics is about how people allocate scarce resources to meet their wants and needs. Factors of production, such as land, labor, and capital, are limited. So businesses decide how to use them. When you earn money, you also have to decide how to allocate your money. By lowering prices, deflation increases your purchasing power. This power is the amount of goods and services that one unit of currency, like a dollar, can buy. When prices decrease, a dollar can buy more goods and services than before. For example, suppose that $1 buys one music download. Then deflation causes

Deflation increases purchasing power. The same amount of money can now buy more goods and services.

the price of music downloads to decrease to 50 cents. After deflation, $1 buys two downloads.

Because your purchasing power increases with deflation, you will need to rethink how to spend, save, or donate your extra money. People often increase their consumption during deflationary periods. This circumstance means using your increased purchasing power to buy more goods and services. You can also choose to put some of your extra money into savings. Budget goals can be short-term, like buying food. They can also be long-term, like purchasing a new computer. Putting some or all of your extra money into savings can help you afford your goals faster. During economic downturns, people choose to save their extra money in case of financial emergencies. Finally, you may opt to donate some of your extra money to charity. There are many worthy causes, such as helping people afford clothes, food, shelter, and medical care. You can use some or all of your extra money to help others, too.

Transferring Wealth

Deflation transfers wealth from borrowers to lenders. Wealth is the value of all tangible assets and productive resources (which can generate current or future income). It includes goods such as houses, cars, and clothes, as well as financial assets, like bank accounts and stocks. Wealth can be calculated by obtaining values for all of these assets and then subtracting any money owed. But deflation affects this equation.

Let's return to Japanese resident Yoshihisa, who bought a $400,000 apartment. After the housing bubble burst and

Japan experienced tangible asset deflation, his apartment was worth only $200,000, but he still owed $300,000 in home loans. His wealth decreased due to deflation because his apartment (and other tangible assets) was worth less than before. If Yoshihisa sold his apartment, he would not have enough money to repay his home debts. Although his apartment is worth less, Yoshihisa still owes the same amount of money as before. In this way, deflation transfers wealth from borrowers (like Yoshihisa) to lenders (such as mortgage brokers and banks who make the loans). Deflation causes borrowers to repay more money compared to the original loan. On the flip side, lenders receive more money than they originally lent.

Suppose that your family owns a home. Deflation hits, and your home is worth less than before. But your parents still have to pay a mortgage based on the original purchase value. So your family's wealth decreases, but your debt is comparatively higher. The good news is that your parents still have their jobs, even though it is a recession. The bad news is that deflation has led to lower wages. Now they have less disposable income to use for bills, such as house expenses. There is also a greater chance of loan defaults, or being unable to legally repay debts.

Business Investments and Deflation

Like consumers, businesses lose wealth with deflation. During economic contractions and deflation, businesses earn lower profits. Profits are calculated as revenues minus costs. Revenues, or money earned from sales, are decreasing

Companies invest in new products because they believe that consumers will buy them. Each year, automobile companies introduce their new cars.

because businesses are making fewer sales and receiving lower prices. But what about their costs? Costs can be variable, which means they change with quantity. They can also be fixed costs, which are costs that exist even without production.

In the auto industry, tires are a variable cost because the cost of tires depends on the number of cars made. Yet the factory building is a fixed cost because its cost is independent of how many cars are manufactured. Businesses make investments, such as taking out loans for factories, and incur fixed costs. These investments are made in the present but are based on future expectations. If a car company opens another factory today, it thinks that demand for cars will remain strong in the future. Deflation can reduce the value of the factory and make the car company owe more money for this asset compared to the initial investment. If businesses expect deflation, they may even choose to delay investments.

During the Great Depression, Irving Fischer developed an economic concept called debt deflation. Debt refers to money owed (like home or factory

Trapped in Reality

Monetary policy is used to maintain price stability. If prices are falling, the Federal Reserve can increase the money supply and lower interest rates. This is supposed to increase consumption and investment, stimulate economic growth, and fight deflation. But contractionary monetary policy does not always work, especially when nominal interest rates are low. Nominal interest rates are the cost of borrowing. Real interest rates are the cost of borrowing, adjusted for the price level. In math terms, real interest is nominal interest minus the inflation rate. But what happens when deflation occurs? Real interest rates are higher than nominal rates.

Suppose that the economy is in a recession. In addition, assume that short-term nominal interest rates are already very low. To encourage more economic growth, the Federal Reserve increases the money supply and lowers interest rates. It hopes that lower interest rates will increase consumer spending and investments. Then the economy can grow and create more jobs. Even so, the Federal Reserve affects the nominal interest rate.

Therefore, even if the Federal Reserve increases the money supply and nominal interest rates fall close to zero, deflation can actually raise real interest rates. Economists David Reifschneider and John C. Williams call this the "deflation trap." It means that the Federal Reserve is ineffective at promoting economic growth in this situation. How does the rise in real interest rates affect consumers like you? It makes spending more expensive. This situation reduces consumption and investment, which discourages economic growth.

loans). Debt deflation occurs when the total debt in the economy is decreasing. In accounting, assets (or items that increase your wealth) equal liabilities (your debts). Liabilities decrease when people pay off their debts or default. When liabilities fall, the value of assets also decreases to maintain balance. This results in falling asset prices, or tangible asset deflation.

Investing Your Money During Deflation

When deflation exists or is expected to occur, there are strategies for earning and protecting your money. Should you put your money into bank accounts, stocks, or bonds? During deflation, cash is the safest investment. It pays to hold cash because deflation increases its purchasing power. Historically, the U.S. dollar has remained

People make investments (like stocks, mutual funds, and real estate) in hope of earning more money. But during deflation, popular investment strategies include holding cash and long-term bonds.

strong during deflationary periods. Another popular place to hold your money is long-term bonds, like U.S. Treasury bonds. A bond is a way for the government and companies to borrow money. Bonds are issued for certain amounts and periods of time. At maturity, a bondholder is repaid the original amount, plus interest.

Stocks are generally not a good investment during deflationary times. As previously discussed, lower prices and sales reduce business profits, increase losses, and reduce stock prices. Commodities, such as gold, can also lose value with deflation. For example, the value of most commodities fell during the Great Depression. Like commodities, real estate loses its value. In fact, some financial advisers recommend renting, rather than buying, a residence. For those who already own a home, it is suggested to pay off as much of their home debts as possible. This also applies to other debts, like credit card bills.

Chapter 5

Preparing for Deflation

Deflation affects you. It can influence your spending decisions, investment choices, employment, income, and loans. The health of the overall economy plays an important role in how you, and others, react to deflation. Actual versus expected deflation, as well as time lags, also influence the impact of deflation. In other words, it is all how you look at it.

Expectations

People and businesses react to what they expect to happen. These expectations are partly formed on present situations but do not always match what actually happens. For example, if people expect prices to fall, they may change their spending habits today. This response can impact consumption and production in the future. Even if deflation does not occur, these consumers' behaviors influence the economy's future.

During deflationary times, people prefer to pay with cash. Incurring credit card debt can decrease the value of your assets while you pay off their original prices.

Businesses then make decisions based on expectations about future economic growth.

Suppose that you expect prices to fall. You may delay your current purchases to take advantage of paying lower prices in the future. You may also choose to pay for any goods and services that you do buy with cash, rather than with credit cards. Remember that deflation transfers wealth from borrowers to lenders. So having debt (such as credit card bills or car, college, or home loans) can lower the value of your assets while making you responsible for their original prices. Expected deflation can also deter you from making big-ticket purchases, like cars, in the near future.

Consumer and business expectations, confidence, and behavior play strong roles in the future levels of economic indicators. The Federal Reserve makes monetary policy decisions based on this data. For example, suppose that the Federal Reserve expects deflation. It increases the money supply and lowers interest rates to counter deflationary fears. Its actions put pressure on prices to rise, as more consumers compete for a limited number of goods and services. As previously discussed, the success of expansionary monetary policy depends on a number of factors, such as the nominal interest rate.

Consider the effects of expansionary monetary policy on consumers like you. Lowering interest rates makes borrowing money less expensive. This encourages you to increase your spending. But if the economy is in a recession and nominal interest rates are already very low, some of the Federal Reserve's actions will be offset by deflation. In other words, real interest rates would rise, which makes borrowing more expensive than the Federal Reserve intended. So consumers

The United States, Japan, and Expectations

In 2001, the United States avoided deflation. The Federal Reserve did engage in expansionary monetary policy. Nevertheless, Federal Reserve chairman Ben Bernanke noted another reason for the country's miss with deflation: consumers' expectations. He cited an October 2002 University of Michigan study that showed consumers expected prices to rise in the future by 2.9 percent. This study was consistent with consumers' expectations in the previous years. If people expected prices to rise, their behaviors would be more consistent with spending choices favorable to inflation. For example, it might put upward pressure on wages (price of labor) so that consumers can afford their current goods and services at higher prices. This behavior counters deflationary pressures.

As noted, the Japanese central bank's reaction to deflation during the lost decade was slow and mild compared to that of the United States. One reason cited by others, including the Federal Reserve, was that the Japanese central bank did not expect deflation. Rather than taking steps to prevent it, the central bank had the job of stopping and reversing deflation once it had begun. The expectations about changes in the price level affect the decisions of consumers and policymakers. What the Japanese central bank, consumers, and businesses were left to deal with was not expected deflation but actual deflation.

like you will not borrow and spend as much as expected because of the expansionary monetary policy.

Consumer Confidence Indicator

How consumers feel about the economy determines their spending and savings habits. For example, consumers who are confident about the economy will buy more goods and services. Their confidence makes them believe that spending today will not affect their abilities to spend tomorrow. As consumers compete for goods and services, this can put pressure on prices to rise and inflation results. But if consumers are not confident about their economic futures, they may spend less and save more. This can put downward pressure on prices and may result in deflation.

The consumer confidence index measures how consumers feel about their current and future economic states. Each month, the Conference Board surveys five thousand households and asks them five questions concerning their feelings about business and employment conditions now and in six months, as well as how they view their family income over the next six months. Businesses, banks, and the government view attitude changes of more than 5 percent as influencing their decisions.

For example, suppose that consumer confidence falls by more than 5 percent, which means that consumers are not confident about their economic futures. This response can result in less spending and more savings. Businesses may react by producing fewer goods and services, cutting costs, and firing workers. Banks may react to an expected decrease

Deflation can affect your spending decisions. During economic growth, lower prices encourage more spending. But during economic contractions, lower prices often do not provide enough incentives to increase spending.

in lending, as consumers reduce big-ticket purchases. The government and Federal Reserve may also engage in expansionary policies to increase spending and investments. These actions put pressure on prices to change. For instance, a decrease in spending may reduce prices, which increases deflationary fears.

Deflation and You

Deflation is about falling prices throughout the economy. How people react to deflation depends on several factors, such as economic growth, job opportunities, consumer confidence, nominal interest rates, and expected future income. Deflation presents opportunities to pay lower prices for goods and services, and it increases your purchasing power. However, consumers may be reluctant to take advantage of better bargains if the economy is contracting and they are worried about their economic futures. Or consumers may simply want to wait until prices fall even more. But sometimes, during economic booms, deflation can encourage people to spend more money.

Deflation also affects you in different ways depending on your role. As a consumer, you want to pay lower prices. But as a worker, you do not want lower wages. Your family may also have debts, such as credit card bills, a mortgage, and college or car loans. In this case, deflation

Your Business

You are a consumer. You purchase goods and services, such as clothes, downloads, and food, in the marketplace. Nonetheless, you may also be a producer. Today, many teens are entrepreneurs. They begin and run businesses while in school. Popular start-ups include selling T-shirts, jewelry, apps, lawn mowing, and dog walking. If deflation hits, it could affect your business, too. You might receive a lower price for your good or service, or you might be reluctant to raise your prices. After all, if people are worried about their own economic futures, they will be less willing to pay more money for your product or service. Moreover, if the prices of other goods and services are decreasing, your product or service looks relatively more expensive—even at its original price.

Another way that deflation might affect your business is through lower input costs. Suppose you make and sell jewelry. Deflation hits and the costs of your materials (such as beads and metal clasps) decrease. This effect means that it costs less to make your product. You can pass along some of these savings to your customers by lowering your prices. This action will help you remain competitive in the marketplace. But suppose that the economy is also in a recession and people are afraid or unable to spend their money. As a result, the demand for your jewelry drops. Now you are selling fewer pieces of jewelry at lower prices. Suddenly, your business does not look so profitable!

will decrease your family's wealth. However, if you have grandparents or know people who receive fixed incomes (for instance, Social Security), their purchasing power just increased. Even though prices have decreased, they receive the same amount of income. Finally, if you own a business, lower prices can affect your input costs and revenues. In other words,

Deflation winners include people with fixed incomes, like those receiving Social Security. These sources of income pay the same amount of money, even as prices are falling.

deflation affects you and others in both positive and negative ways at the same time, like lowering prices and your wages.

When you hear about the threat or existence of deflation, pay attention to how the Federal Reserve and government react. Their actions affect you. For example, the nominal cost of borrowing money becomes less expensive when the Federal Reserve increases the money supply. Expansionary policies aimed at controlling or preventing deflation often affect economic growth, which means your job market. Increased growth provides more jobs. It also encourages more consumer spending, including more demand for your products. No matter what your role or the policy, remember that cash holds the most purchasing power in times of deflation. "Cash is king" is the rule.

GLOSSARY

allocate To distribute resources or duties for a particular purpose.

central bank A country's main bank that controls the money supply, issues currency, and supervises commercial banks.

consumption The value of goods and services bought by individuals.

deceleration A decrease in the growth rate.

deflation A persistent decline in the general prices of goods and services.

demand The amount of goods and services that people are willing and able to buy.

disposable income Money earned after deductions, such as taxes.

fiscal policy A government's use of spending and taxes intended to affect economic performance.

inflation A sustained increase in the general prices of goods and services.

interest The cost of borrowing money; a lender's rate of return.

investment The act of putting money into something with the hope of earning more money.

loan default The failure to repay money that is legally owed.

monetary policy A central bank's use of money supply and interest rates to affect economic growth and price stability.

money supply The amount of money in the economy at a certain time.

purchasing power The amount of goods and services that one unit of currency, like a dollar, can buy.

recession When total output, often measured as gross domestic product, falls, usually for at least six months.

revenue Money received from the sales of goods and services.

risk averse Preferring a more certain outcome to an uncertain one.

Standard & Poor's A stock market index.

tax A government fee on items, such as income and goods.

unemployment A state in which working-age people who want to work and are actively looking are unable to find jobs.

wage An income earned from working.

wealth The value of all tangible assets and productive resources.

FOR MORE INFORMATION

Bank of Canada
234 Wellington Street
Ottawa, ON K1A 0G9
Canada
(613) 782-8111
Web site: http://www.bankofcanada.ca
The Bank of Canada is the central bank of Canada. Its
    duties include carrying out monetary policy through
    open-market operations.

Board of Governors of the Federal Reserve System
Twentieth Street and Constitution Avenue NW
Washington, DC 20551
Web site: http://www.federalreserve.gov
The Federal Reserve is the United States' central bank. Its
    responsibilities include controlling the money supply,
    supervising and regulating banks, providing financial
    services, and maintaining financial stability.

Department of Finance Canada
East Tower, 19th Floor
140 O'Connor Street
Ottawa, ON K1A 0G5
Canada
(613) 992-1573
Web site: http://www.fin.gc.ca/fin-eng.asp
The Department of Finance Canada prepares the Canadian

federal government's budget, which documents government revenue and expenses.

Internal Revenue Service (IRS)
U.S. Department of the Treasury
1500 Pennsylvania Avenue NW
Washington, DC 20220
(800) 829-1040
Web site: http://www.irs.gov
The IRS is a U.S. government agency that collects taxes
and enforces tax laws. It provides information on filing
taxes and reports changes in the tax structure, such as
new tax credits.

National Bureau of Economic Research (NBER)
1050 Massachusetts Avenue
Cambridge, MA 02138
(617) 868-3900
Web site: http://www.nber.org
The NBER is a research organization that studies how the
economy works, including the effects of deflation.

Office of Management and Budget (OMB)
725 Seventeenth Street NW
Washington, DC 20503
(202) 395-3080
Web site: http://www.whitehouse.gov/omb

The OMB is the largest component of the Executive Office of the President. It is responsible for developing and carrying out the federal budget.

U.S. Department of Labor
200 Constitution Avenue NW
Washington, DC 20210
(866) 487-2365 or (877) 889-5627
Web site: http://www.dol.gov
The U.S. Department of Labor reports data on price changes, such as those measured by the consumer price index. It is also a resource for wage earners, job seekers, and retirees.

Web Sites

Due to the changing nature of Internet links, Rosen Publishing has developed an online list of Web sites related to the subject of this book. This site is updated regularly. Please use this link to access the list:

http://www.rosenlinks.com/YEF/Defla

FOR FURTHER READING

Axilrod, Stephen H. *Inside the Fed: Monetary Policy and Its Management, Martin Through Greenspan to Bernanke.* Cambridge, MA: MIT Press, 2009.

Bernstein, Peter L., and Paul A. Volcker. *A Primer on Money, Banking, and Gold.* Hoboken, NJ: Wiley, 2008.

Brezina, Corona. *How Deflation Works.* New York, NY: Rosen Publishing, 2010.

Brinton, Mary C. *Lost in Transition: Youth, Work, and Instability in Postindustrial Japan.* Cambridge, MA: Cambridge University Press, 2010.

Dheeriya, Prakash L. *Finance for Kidz.* Rancho Palos Verde, CA: Fintelligence Publishing, 2010.

Flynn, Sean Masaki. *Economics for Dummies.* Hoboken, NJ: Wiley, 2011.

Gorman, Tom. *The Complete Idiot's Guide to Economics.* New York, NY: Alpha Books, 2011.

Hamada, Koichi, Kazumasa Iwata, Anil K. Kashyap, and David E. Weinstein. *Japan's Bubble, Deflation, and Long-term Stagnation.* Cambridge, MA: MIT Press, 2010.

Krantz, Katherine, and Francois Trahan. *The Era of Uncertainty: Global Investment Strategies for Inflation, Deflation, and the Middle Ground.* Hoboken, NJ: Wiley, 2011.

Mauldin, John, and Jonathan Tepper. *Endgame: The End of the Debt Supercycle and How It Changes Everything.* Hoboken, NJ: Wiley, 2011.

Minden, Cecilia. *Understanding Taxes.* Ann Arbor, MI: Cherry Lake Publishing, 2009.

Moss, David A. *A Concise Guide to Macroeconomics: What Managers, Executives, and Students Need to Know.* Cambridge, MA: Harvard Business School Press, 2007.

Piper, Mike. *Taxes Made Simple: Income Taxes Explained in 100 Pages or Less.* Chicago, IL: Simple Subjects, 2009.

Prechter, Robert R., Jr. *Conquer the Crash: You Can Survive and Prosper in a Deflationary Depression.* Hoboken, NJ: Wiley, 2003.

Saxonhouse, Gary, and Robert Stern. *Japan's Lost Decade: Origins, Consequences, and Prospects for Recovery.* Malden, MA: Blackwell Publishers, 2004.

Schiff, Andrew J., and Peter D. Schiff. *How an Economy Grows and Why It Crashes.* Hoboken, NJ: Wiley, 2010.

Shaffer, Daniel S. *Profiting in Economic Storms: A Historic Guide to Surviving Depression, Deflation, Hyperinflation, and Market Bubbles.* Hoboken, NJ: Wiley, 2010.

Tanaka, Graham. *Digital Deflation.* New York, NY: McGraw-Hill, 2008.

Wiegand, Steve. *Lessons from the Great Depression for Dummies.* Hoboken, NJ: Wiley, 2009.

Wild, Russell. *Bond Investing for Dummies.* Hoboken, NJ: Wiley, 2007.

BIBLIOGRAPHY

Bernanke, Ben S. "Deflation: Making Sure 'It' Doesn't Happen Here." Federal Reserve Board, November 21, 2002. Retrieved January 20, 2012 (http://www .federalreserve.gov/boarddocs/speeches/2002/ 20021121/default.htm).

Bloomberg Businessweek. "Japan's Lost Generation." May 28, 2007. Retrieved January 30, 2012 (http://www. businessweek.com/magazine/content/07_22/ b4036068.htm).

Brooks, Douglas H., and Pilipinas F. Quising. "Dangers of Deflation." Asian Development Bank, December 2002. Retrieved January 8, 2012 (http://www.adb.org/ Documents/EDRC/Policy_Briefs/PB012.pdf).

Burdekin, Richard C. K., and Pierre L. Siklos. *Deflation: Current and Historical Perspectives* (Studies in Macroeconomic History). Cambridge, England: Cambridge University Press, 2010.

Bureau of Labor Statistics. "Table 1A. Consumer Price Index for All Urban Consumers (CPI-U)." Retrieved January 12, 2012 (http://www.bls.gov/cpi/cpid09av.pdf).

Davis, Matthew. "Fighting Deflation in the U.S. and Japan." National Bureau of Economic Research. Retrieved January 14, 2012 (http://www.nber.org/digest/jun05/ w10938.html).

Dotzour, Mark G., and Gerald Klassen. "Inflation and Deflation." Real Estate Center at Texas A & M University, October 2010. Retrieved January 14, 2012 (http://recenter.tamu.edu/pdf/1946.pdf).

The Economist. "Deflation in America: The Greater of Two Evils." May 7, 2009. Retrieved January 15, 2012 (http://www.economist.com/node/13610845).

Fackler, Martin. "Take It from Japan: Bubbles Hurt." *New York Times,* December 25, 2005. Retrieved January 15, 2012 (http://www.nytimes.com/2005/12/25/business/yourmoney/25japan.html?pagewanted=all).

Federal Reserve Bank of San Francisco. "About the Fed: What Are Real Interest Rates and Why Do They Matter?" Retrieved January 16, 2012 (http://www.frbsf.org/publications/federalreserve/monetary/affect.html).

Federal Reserve Bank of San Francisco. "Understanding Deflation." Economic Research and Data, April 2, 2004. Retrieved January 16, 2012 (http://www.frbsf.org/publications/economics/letter/2004/el2004-08.html).

Fisher, Irving. *The Debt-Deflation Theory of Great Depressions.* Seattle, WA: CreateSpace, 2012.

Foley, Stephen. "Oil Price Fall Sees Deflation Return to U.S. for First Time Since 1955." *Independent,* April 16, 2009. Retrieved January 17, 2012 (http://www.independent.co.uk/news/business/news/oil-price-fall-sees-deflation-return-to-us-for-first-time-since-1955-1669375.html).

Global Property Guide. "Quake-Traumatized Japanese Shun Condos." January 25, 2012. Retrieved January 26, 2012 (http://www.globalpropertyguide.com/Asia/Japan/Price-History).

Hollander, Barbara Gottfried. *Booms, Bubbles, & Busts: The Economic Cycle.* Chicago, IL: Heinemann Library, 2011.

Hollander, Barbara Gottfried. *Money Matters: An Introduction to Economics.* Chicago, IL: Heinemann Library, 2011.

Kaza, Greg. '"Deflation and Economic Growth." *Quarterly Journal of Austrian Economics*, Vol. 9, No. 2, Summer 2006. Retrieved January 17, 2012 (http://mises.org/journals/qjae/pdf/qjae9_2_5.pdf).

Market Folly. "Best Investments During Deflation." August 9, 2010. Retrieved January 18, 2012 (http://www.marketfolly.com/2010/08/best-investments-during-deflation.html).

RandomHistory.com. "50 Interesting Facts About the Great Depression." April 12, 2009. Retrieved January 18, 2012 (http://facts.randomhistory.com/2009/04/12_great-depression.html).

Reinhart, Vincent R. "The Deflation Club." *The American: The Online Magazine of the American Enterprise Institute*, April 27, 2010. Retrieved January 18, 2012 (http://www.american.com/archive/2010/april/the-deflation-club).

Schwartz, Nelson D. "Spain's Falling Prices Fuel Deflation Fears in Europe." *New York Times*, April 20, 2009. Retrieved January 18, 2012 (http://www.nytimes.com/2009/04/21/business/global/21deflate.html?ref=deflationeconomics).

Shilling, A. Gary. "Deflation Has Arrived." Forbes.com, October 5, 2011. Retrieved January 17, 2012 (http://www.forbes.com/forbes/2011/1024/opinions-investing-deflation-arrived-markets-Bernanke-federal-open-committee-gary-shilling.html).

Shilling, A. Gary. *Deflation: How to Survive & Thrive in the Coming Wave of Deflation.* New York, NY: McGraw-Hill, 2002.

SurePayroll.com. "Salary Paycheck Calculator." Retrieved January 15, 2012 (http://www.surepayroll.com/calculator/calc_paycheck_netpay.asp).

Trading Economics. "Japan Inflation Rate." Retrieved February 1, 2012 (http://www.tradingeconomics.com/japan/inflation-cpi).

World Bank. "Inflation, Consumer Prices (Annual %)." Retrieved January 30, 2012 (http://data.worldbank.org/indicator/FP.CPI.TOTL.ZG?page=3).

About the Author

Barbara Gottfried Hollander has authored several economics and business books, including *How Credit Crises Happen*, *Money Matters: An Introduction to Economics*, *How Currency Devaluation Works*, and *Booms, Bubbles, & Busts: The Economic Cycle*. She is an economic content developer and specialized project manager for online education companies. Hollander was the economics editor of the *World Almanac and Book of Facts*, where she analyzed statistical data on economic indicators and the performances of world economies. She received a B.A. degree in economics from the University of Michigan and an M.A. degree in economics from New York University.

Photo Credits

Cover (sign) © iStockphoto.com/Tim McCaig; cover (ragged paper) © iStockphoto.com/Petek Arici p. 4 Seth Joel/Photographer's Choice RF/Getty Images; pp. 8–9, 14–15 Justin Sullivan/Getty Images; p. 17 Remi Benali/Gamma-Rapho/Getty Images; pp. 22–23 © iStockphoto.com/ Kenneth Sponsler; p. 26 Kzenon/Shutterstock.com; pp. 28–29, 44–45 © AP Images; p. 32 John Grant/Photographer's Choice/Getty Images; pp. 34–35 Bloomberg/Getty Images; pp. 40–41 Ethan Miller/Getty Images; pp. 46 Spencer Platt/Getty Images; p. 49 Ariel Skelley/Blend Images/Getty Images; pp. 52–53 © Jim West/Report Digital-REA/Redux; p. 55 © iStockphoto.com/Walter Galloway; p. 58 JupiterImages/Brand X Pictures/Thinkstock; pp. 62–63 pryzmat/Shutterstock; p. 65 Jack Hollingsworth/Photodisc/Thinkstock; (background graphic) pp. 7, 21, 38, 48, 57 © iStockphoto.com/Ivan Blitznetsov.

Designer: Michael Moy; Editor: Kathy Kuhtz Campbell;
Photo Researcher: Marty Levick